Oldham
Inspirational Library
Volume 2

Living Close
to God

By W. Dale Oldham

Large-Print
Abridged Edition

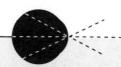

**This Large Print Book carries the
Seal of Approval of N.A.V.H.**
National Association for Visually Handicapped

Warner Press
Anderson, Indiana

Coordinator of Communications and Publishing
Church of God Ministries, Inc.
PO Box 2420, Anderson, IN 46018-2420
800-848-2464 • www.chog.org

To purchase additional copies of this book, to inquire about distribution and for all other sales-related matters, please contact:

 Warner Press, Inc.
PO Box 2499, Anderson, IN 46018-9988
877-346-3974 • www.warnerpress.com

Text abridgement: Joseph D. Allison
Cover design: Carolyn A. Frost
ISBN 978-1-59317-177-3

Library of Congress Cataloging-in-Publication Data

Oldham, Dale.
    Living close to God / by W. Dale Oldham. -- Large-print abridged ed.
       p.   cm. -- (Oldham inspirational library ; v. 2)
    ISBN 978-1-59317-177-3 (pbk.)
    1. Christian life. I. Title.
  BV4501.3.O456 2007
  248.4--dc22   2007015896

Printed in the United States of America
07 08 09 10 11 / EP / 10 9 8 7 6 5 4 3 2 1

Table of Contents

*This book is lovingly dedicated
to Polly,
whose godly aspirations have
whetted my own.*

Foreword

I know Dr. Oldham personally, have been greatly blessed by his friendship, and challenged by his knowledge of God and his ability to communicate that knowledge. *Living Close to God* has added a new dimension. I have been set free in a new way. I no longer merely admire Dale Oldham's sincere and productive life, and rejoice in my friendship with him and his beloved Polly. I have heard new heavenly laughter and feel a new longing within myself to know Jesus Christ as he really is!

I believe my experience will be yours as you read through the forcefully written pages of this book. You will see that no one, not even a great preacher, has a "corner on the market" of the victorious life in Christ! You will see Christ as he is. Your heart will ache to know him better. You will come to see that the genuine disciple of Jesus Christ is never dissatisfied, but always unsatisfied!

You will realize this and rejoice in your realization as you come to see that nothing merits our gratitude as much as to see our own desperate need and the face of the only One who can fill it!

In this unusual book, Dale Oldham turns from his position as a needy disciple to that of a dedicated, clear-thinking minister of the gospel. He shows us how to lay hold of God's grace. He shows us God's part and our part with magnificent balance. He reminds us (and I rejoice in this!) that if even Judas had been willing to repent, Jesus would have forgiven him!

Dr. Oldham testifies that he is "singing more and [being] irritated less" since he has become convinced that all fullness is in the person of Jesus Christ. This is my own experience too, and it has been deepened and heightened since I have read *Living Close to God*.

Eugenia Price
Chicago, Illinois

Publisher's Preface

In the fall of 1963, Dr. Dale Oldham was preaching for a series of revival services in Huntington, Indiana. The soloist for the week was his son, Doug Oldham, accompanied by a young pianist named Bill Gaither.

On their way home that Saturday night, they talked about what was happening. Dr. Oldham said, "Bill, there's something about that word *touch*. You ought to write a song about how God touches lives."*

Early the next morning, Gaither sat down at a piano and wrote a song titled "He Touched Me." Doug Oldham sang it in the revival service that morning. Soon other musicians began singing it, because people were eager to hear the message it conveyed: Jesus Christ can entirely change a person's life. Not the teachings of Jesus, the lifestyle of Jesus, or the religion of Jesus — Jesus

---

*Bill Gaither and Ken Abraham, It's More Than the Music (New York: Time Warner, 2003), 75.

himself changes lives. No matter how desperate we feel, we have hope because we can have a personal relationship with the Son of God.

That message was the theme of Dale Oldham's preaching throughout his ministry. In this book, he shows us that it's the secret of vital Christianity.

If Christianity were nothing more than a system of beliefs or an affiliation with a like-minded group, our spiritual lives would grow stale. But it's more than that. It's a personal relationship with Jesus Christ, who sends his Spirit to live within us.

We have abridged Dr. Oldham's text to accommodate this large-print format, but his message is vibrant as ever. May it draw you nearer to the heart of God.

1. The Quest Begins

Some of us, although we have been Christians for many years, still hunger and thirst for that which is above and beyond anything we have yet attained in Christ. We yearn to know Christ better, to be more like him. How grateful we are for the heavenly aspirations that flood our souls! Thank God for a hunger that is never fully satisfied! Thank God we still thirst after the righteousness that is by faith! St. Augustine was right in saying that God made us for himself and our souls are restless until they rest in him. None but God can satisfy the inner cravings of the human heart; none but he can provide the peace that passes all understanding.

All who share this quest for spiritual growth can say with the psalmist, " As a deer longs for flowing streams, so my soul longs for you, O God. My soul thirsts for God, for the living God" (Ps 42:1–2). Why does something within us remain unsatisfied even when our sins have been confessed and by faith we have accepted the Savior's pardon? How can we be "filled" and yet remain unsatisfied? How can we drink daily from the flowing fountain of God's love and grace yet still thirst?

It all amounts to this: To thirst for God means to thirst for everything God loves. God loves world order. Do you thirst for that? God loves social justice, righteousness, purity, truth, and a forgiving spirit. Do you thirst for all these? God loves those who are dedicated to the highest and best for others. Are you so dedicated? God loves obedient servants who render Christian service in love. Are you one of these?

"My soul thirsts for God!" How soul-searching are the implications of this simple phrase! Do we thirst for Christ's saving power to be experienced in all the earth? Or are we so enamored of our own little circumscribed environment that we can

2

neither hear the cries of the distressed nor see their wretchedness and poverty?

You can't actually thirst for God unless you first believe in God with your whole heart. Let childhood ideas about God give way to more mature concepts of deity. God is love as well as justice. His love endures forever (Ps 100:5). He receives no pleasure from the chastening of evil men nor in the death of the wicked (Ezek 33:11). Jesus said, "Whoever has seen me has seen the Father" (John 14:9). If God is like Jesus, we have in the Master a splendid picture of him.

An adult sense of God, combined with a deep love and devotion to him and to all for which he stands, opens the doorway to a more vital relationship with Christ and his people. There is power for meaningful living as we understand God better. Henry Drummond said it was this sense of God in his life that gave him a new standard of values by which to judge life. Wilfred T. Grenfell said that his university and professional experience took on a new meaning when he discovered this "center of moral oughtness." To grow spiritually, we must grow up in our theology.

Much that is supposed to be religious faith is altogether too shallow and weak to bring deep satisfaction to the human heart. What good is a form of godliness if there is too little of genuine piety, too little devotion to duty and truth, too much dilution of the Spirit of Christ in one's life? John R. Mott once said with keen insight, "An alarming weakness among Christians is that we are producing Christian activities faster than we are producing Christian experience and Christian faith."[1] Today's Christians possess many skills—we can organize, advertise, promote, and execute our programs with dispatch—but do we have the Spirit of Christ? Do we possess a living, vital, dynamic faith in God? Are we utterly surrendered to his will? Do we seek first the kingdom of God and his righteousness?

---

1. John R. Mott, introduction, *The Meaning of Prayer,* by Harry Emerson Fosdick (New York: Abingdon Press: 1915).

Sometimes it is extremely hard to see God. The world is too much with us. Its noise and clanging strife are all about us. Its raucous voices are forever demanding to be heard. Surrounded by such an environment, it is possible to become confused and lose your bearings.

In this world of sin and evil, of pain and war, of frustration and disappointment, we cannot always be cloistered in the quiet hush of a church or hidden away in our very own secret place of prayer. Neither can we always hear the voice nor feel the touch of God's divine hand. But if our sensitivity to spiritual values has been increased by daily proximity to the throne, we will be able to steer along that shore that marks God's holy will for our lives. God still makes his will known to the pure in heart.

With this opening chapter we begin our quest together for a closer walk with God. Be assured, he wants us to enjoy that closer walk! He promises growth and grace to the

humble—to all those who, with the psalmist, earnestly cry, "My soul thirsts for God,
for the living God " (Ps 42:2)

---

2. To Be Like Him

One primary aim of Christian devotion is personal godliness—to be
like Christ. Is this possible, or has
God created us with a tormenting hunger
and thirst for righteousness only to turn us
away unsatisfied?

Jesus prayed, "And this is eternal life,
that they may know you, the only true God,
and Jesus Christ whom you have sent"
(John 17:3). And in John 14:9, we find Jesus
saying to Philip (as quoted previously),
"Whoever has seen me has seen the Father." So if we can know Jesus, we can also
know the Father. Yet to really know Jesus,
one must become like him.

Some time ago I determined to find a richer and more satisfying walk with God. Although I had been a Christian since the age of sixteen, there was the feeling that my relationship with Jesus Christ ought to be providing more for my life than was apparently there. So over the intervening months, I have been praying earnestly (and, I think, honestly) for advancement in my own spiritual life. That longing has finally resolved itself into a great yearning for a person—and that person is Christ!

This new direction has changed my prayer habits radically. Formerly, much of my praying was an effort to beg from God the attributes of Christ. Now the prayer is for Christ himself to be mine in a new way, whereby he can control me more fully; for if Christ is mine, all else I need will be provided. New meaning has come to Romans 8:32, where Paul assured the Christians at Rome, "He who did not withhold his own Son, but gave him up for all of us, will he not with him also give us everything else?"

The Revised Standard Version gives that last phrase as, "Will he not also give us all things with him?"

The attributes of Christ will follow Christ into your heart. Don't pray for patience: pray for Christ, for when he is enthroned upon the high place of your heart, you will have patience. Instead of praying for control, make full room for Christ and he will provide control. When I ceased praying for love, faith, and other Christlike virtues, and began seeking instead a warm companionship with Christ, I experienced an infilling of these neglected qualities, which I trust will never cease. Out of the experience of these months — really, a period of a couple of years — has come a "magnificent obsession" for Christ himself.

Years ago, Polly and I gave our son Doug to a lovely girl in marriage. A year or two prior to that time, we had not known this girl existed. Then we gave her our son. How many, many more things we have given her in the intervening years! Why? Because we first gave her our son.

When God gives you his Son, he will follow that gift with everything you really need, if you but trust his grace and are obedient to his will.

Words fail me in conveying to you what has taken place in my heart. All I can say is this: I want Christ in his sacred fullness to be sovereign Lord of my life, to be with me every waking moment. I want this more than I have ever wanted anything in my life. I want to be like him at any cost.

I am so deep into confession already that I may as well be even a bit more personal, and in this I beg your forgiveness. I have been married for more than thirty years to the lovely, most charming woman to whom this book is dedicated. Some of you have surmised how deeply I am devoted to this companion who has stood so loyally by my side through the heavy and long years of an exceedingly busy ministry. To me, there is no one like her in all the world. Just to be with her brings relaxation and contentment. I believe I could live serenely on a desert island if we were together. I revel in her confidence and trust. The touch of her hand still thrills me. It would break my heart to disappoint her or do anything that would hurt her.

I did not tell you these things to be melodramatic or sentimental, but to prepare this analogy: My feelings for Christ are just like the feelings for my wife, but even more so. How can I explain it further to you? Some of you already know this warm, thrilling relationship to Christ. We rejoice in his friendship and hope for his confidence. For us to deliberately hurt him or sin against him is unthinkable. We long to saturate our souls in him forever!

Oh, I struggled so long! The struggle is hard when we try to do in our own strength something that Christ alone can do for us. Yet victory is comparatively easy and simple when you have found the way. You merely give up your personal sovereignty and let Christ take over. I mean this. It is just that simple. It is easy or hard to do, according to whether or not you actually want Christ to have his way in your life.

You must experience what psychologists call "the expulsive power of a new affection." In other words, you must undergo the crucifixion of the carnal self so that the thoroughly Christianized self may come to expression.

A little girl awoke one morning, sat up in bed, and gazed into a mirror hanging on the opposite wall. In the mirror, she could see reflected plainly a picture of Jesus that hung on the wall above the head of her bed. Noticing this for the first time, she exclaimed, "Mother, I can see Jesus in the mirror." To get a better view, she decided to stand up, but this brought her body between the picture and the mirror and Christ was shut out. This interested the little girl, and she had to stand and lie down several times, experimenting with her new discovery. Finally, she said, "Mother, when I can't see myself, I can see Jesus; but every time I see myself, I can't see him." It is too bad all of us don't realize this.

We stand in front of the cross or behind it. We either exhibit Christ or hide him. When Christ is made sovereign, he controls our lives. He gives the orders. He provides the divine stimulus, the holy impulse, the godly motivation for our lives.

---

3. The Life Worthy of God

In writing to the church at Thessalonica, the apostle Paul said, "As you know, we dealt with each one of you like a father with his children, urging and encouraging you and pleading that you lead a life worthy of God" (1 Thess 2:11–12). "Prove yourselves worthy of your family name," or, "Prove worthy of our great institutions." Instead he said, "Lead a life worthy of God."

It is so easy to confuse truth and tradition, to think we are being loyal to God because we are loyal to a particular movement or organization. However, Christ is our perfect example. Although he was a Jew, he was loyal to Judaism only when Judaism was loyal to truth. So we dare not say, "My church, right or wrong." Paul did not.

Anyone who would live close to God must have a life patterned after Christ himself — his unswerving devotion to truth, his undeviating commitment to principle, his flawless morality, his unimpeachable goodness, his spotless innocence. For in Christ, "the Word became flesh and lived among us" (John 1:14). In him, "the whole fullness of deity dwells bodily "(Col 2:9).

He was gentle, but bold as a lion; confident, yet humble in the presence of God; wise with the wisdom of the ages, and yet his entire life was characterized by an amazing simplicity. He met crises with calmness, trouble with fortitude, hate with forgiveness, disloyalty with a magnanimous spirit, crucifixion with an undying faith. No man ever possessed a truer sense of values. When he said, "Follow me," he spoke not only to his disciples but to all of us—to you and me. Following him means living a life fully dedicated to God.

To live a life worthy of God, we must follow Christ in humble ways of Christian service. How many thousands of dedicated Christians have gone all out to make converts to the faith! They have plunged into steaming jungles, crossed frozen mountains and burning deserts, faced deprivation and persecution, traversed continents, and sailed the seven seas on behalf of Christ. They imitated God's Son in their restless desire to take all the gospel to all the people.

Can we match their zeal and crusading spirit? Will we infiltrate every segment of society with the gospel until individual lives, governments, and social and political processes become thoroughly Christian? God walks in dangerous places. Do we have the courage to follow?

14

Years ago, an Englishman found the secret of a worthy life. He was a plain Methodist minister who fell in love with Christ's goodness and mercy, whose heart was touched like Christ's with the needs of humanity. He went down into the poverty-stricken East End of London and spent days with the unlovely and broken who lived there. At home, he said to his wife one evening, "Darling, I have given myself, you and the children, to the service of these sick souls." His wife instantly agreed to his commitment. Hand in hand they prayed, and in that humble act, a new world of service was opened to them. The man was William Booth, and with this acceptance of his God-given responsibility, the Salvation Army was born.

To be worthy of God, we must give ourselves to accomplishing the tasks begun on earth by Christ. Those tasks wait for completion by members of his Body — by you and me.

4. Marks of Spiritual Maturity

The patriarch Jacob deceived his father, took advantage of his brother in a sly business deal, and then had to flee his home to save his life. Trying to escape the wrath of his brother, Jacob journeyed toward Haran as night overtook him. Exhausted, he lay down upon the ground with a stone for a pillow. As he slept, he dreamed of a ladder that reached from earth to heaven. Angels were ascending and descending this ladder, and above all was God.

Anyone who would live closer to God also has a ladder to climb. How far we climb, or how fast, is entirely up to us. We are not commanded, but invited, to climb. Our spiritual development is determined by the strength of our determination and the quality of our love. Some Christians seem content to spend their lives on the lowest rung of the ladder, but others begin to climb the moment a way of growth is opened to them.

So what is the first step of spiritual progress in the Christian life? Surely not a knowledge of Christian doctrine, for there is something even more basic — the possession of the Spirit of Christ. This is the trademark of a Christian, regardless of all other attainments, and there is no substitute for it. Paul wrote, "Anyone who does not have the Spirit of Christ does not belong to him" (Rom 8:9). Christians are known by their Christlike spirit. The very word *Christian* means "Christlike."

Having received the Spirit of Christ, we must have certain basic convictions — convictions based on a thorough study of the Bible. There is no shortcut to this, nor should any be desired. A handed-down theology, separate and apart from personal study of the Scriptures, will never be fully satisfying. One ought to excavate these diamonds of holy truth for oneself.

Many Christians have but a sketchy idea of what constitutes genuine Christian beliefs. They have opinions and are quick to defend them, but mere opinions are easily refuted. We need solid convictions based upon the unchanging truth of God's eternal Word. Paul wrote to Titus, "But as for you, teach what is consistent with sound doctrine " (2:1). How can we teach others what we have not learned?

The next rung on our ladder of growth is called faith, for "without faith it is impossible to please God" (Heb 11:6). Strong discipleship will be characterized by a strong Christian faith. Yes, it is possible to know the truth but have little faith; some Christians entertain deep convictions but are unwilling to follow them. However, it is not enough to know the truth; we must obey it. It is not enough for divine light to shine on our pathway; we must have the faith to step boldly out into it.

Christian faith entails much more than the belief that God will hear and answer prayer. Christian faith is a way of life. It motivates our every choice and determines the direction we will take down through the years. It is the basis for Christian hope; it keeps us from despairing, regardless of circumstances.

Faith insists that God is still on his throne, even when all is not right with the world. This faith becomes the set of the Christian mind. It believes, not blindly, but with reason, that no matter how dark the night, the sun will shine again; no matter how long the conflict, right will ultimately triumph; no matter how rampant the powers of evil, righteousness will have the final word.

A woman apologized for the condition of her tarnished silver tea service. As she took it from the cabinet, she said, "It's awfully tarnished. I don't use it enough to keep it bright." Faith is like that: To be kept bright, it must be used. Live your faith every day. Step out boldly as your light advances.

You take another step upward in your Christian progress when you begin to carry a burden for others, when you bring the needs of others to the throne of God in prayer. You are even more mature when you begin to pray that Christ will bring new life to a sinner. You ascend still higher when you set yourself to win that soul to God.

A certain pastor became discouraged because no one had been converted in his church for a considerable length of time. In this mood, he tendered his resignation to the congregation. In the official board meeting that followed, different members urged him to stay on, insisting that they were always edified by his preaching. He retorted, "Edified for what?" Turning to one of his leading laymen, the pastor asked, "Have you ever won a soul to Christ?" The layman hung his head. The minister insisted on asking the same question of every person present, all of whom were persons in the church. None had ever won a single person to Christ. Finally, the pastor persuaded these leaders to agree to a proposition: They would all resign if they brought no one to the Lord in the next thirty days. The very next day, one of these men led his business associate to the Lord. By the following Sunday, this man alone had brought in ten more. In four weeks, this previously inactive group of lay leaders had won thirty souls to Christ.

A healthy Christian is a soul winner. Never cease to pray and work for the transformation of others — those who are missing the way of life. You grow up in God as you carry a burden for them. Be true to your trust. The worst profligate can be made into a saint. The most self-righteous hypocrite can be awakened. The members of your own family can be won to Christ. Try it!

Another rung on the ladder of spiritual maturity is sensitivity to God's guidance. This doesn't come naturally. You need to seek God's guidance and follow the guidance you receive.

From the inner precincts of New York Harbor out through the Narrows, where deep water begins, stretches Ambrose Channel, sixteen miles long. The channel is not very wide, however. In bygone days, it was very difficult to navigate in fog or storm. Then the Port Authority laid a cable up the center of the channel, energizing it with alternating electrical current, which can be detected by each ship. The strength of these signals tells a pilot when the ship is directly above the cable and can thus make the passage safely. No matter how dark the night of your understanding or how thick the fog of your circumstances, spiritual progress is possible. The still, small voice of God can always be heard by the sensitive spirit of a dedicated Christian. You need never lose your way.

You can make constant progress on your Christian journey. Better still, by God's help, you can gather up others and take them with you.

22

5. Further Steps in Discipleship

We want to grow in God's grace. We want today's best to become tomorrow's starting point. No Christian need apologize for desiring to be a better person.

This world is pretty hard on perfectionists. To be a Christian does not mean you are incapable of blundering or error. We are still human beings who must occasionally humble ourselves to say, "I'm sorry; please forgive me." Perhaps it is the presence of Christ that gives necessary grace to make the apology.

If victory is interrupted by temporary defeat, remember 1 John 2:1, "But if anyone does sin, we have an advocate with the Father, Jesus Christ the righteous." To stumble is one thing; to stay down is another. Peter, James, and John failed Jesus lamentably in the garden of Gethsemane, and that failure could have ruined them for life, had they permitted it to do so. But they righted themselves, turned their backs on failure, and went on to success for God.

Some Christians make slow progress in their walk with God because they lack gratitude. The redeemed heart should be a grateful heart. We do have so much for which to be grateful. The work of redemption does far more than save the soul. The past is forgiven, the present is illuminated, and the future is insured. Our spirits are liberated and then inspired by the gift of God's righteousness and free grace. Never fail to be thankful to God for what he has done for you, and put your thanks into words at every opportunity. The thankful heart is the safe heart.

Someone has said that gratitude is the mother of all virtues. If so, gratitude and humility are twin brothers; where one is, the other is generally to be found. Thankfulness is a natural fruit of our new life in Christ. If it is true that we are not our own, that we are bought with a price (1 Cor 6:19–20), then we should give the rest of our lives in an effort to repay God the debt we owe. Yet what can we give that we have not received from God's bountiful hand? As the hymn by William W. How has it,

> We give Thee but Thine own,
> Whate'er the gift may be;
> All that we have is Thine alone,
> A trust, O Lord, from Thee.

Obedience accompanies gratitude to God. In John 15:10, Jesus said, "If you keep my commandments, you will abide in my love." Obedience is fundamental to Christian growth.

So if you would live close to God, remember these five steps: First, recognize your incompleteness without God. Second, frankly face any recurring cause for guilt. Third, place your unswerving faith in Christ as your Savior and Keeper. Fourth, continually express your gratitude for redemption and all other divine blessings. And last, render your unquestioning obedience to all of God's commands. Then you can say with Paul, "Not that I have already obtained this or have already reached the goal; but I press on to make it my own, because Christ Jesus has made me his own. Beloved, do not consider that I have made it my own; but this one thing I do: forgetting what lies behind and straining forward to what lies ahead, I press on toward the goal for the prize of the heavenly call of God in Christ Jesus" (Phil 3:12–14).

An old man was mixing mortar for the construction of a beautiful building. It was menial labor, and he was often wearied by it. On the wall of the little cubicle that served as a construction office hung the architect's sketch of the building as it would appear when finished. Every morning as he came to work, the old man stopped to view this picture. As he worked on through the long hours of the day, his thoughts would stray from the scattered materials, the dirt and the mud, the piles of brick and lumber, to firmly recall the beautiful picture of the finished structure. It gave him strength to continue his labor and helped to assure the building's final beauty.

Great lives begin with God-inspired dreams. Your high ideals are a gift from God. Keep them intact, remembering that each is a heaven-sent challenge to stay at your best. As you stand beside your Lord, his divinity strongly accentuates your humanity. Your dedicated humanity is in turn molded into godly patterns by his gracious presence.

Keep growing day after day, claiming victory through grace and faith. Refuse to capitulate to the evil all about you. Earnestly look forward to the day when your faith will be lost in sight — when your humanity will be swallowed up forever in Christ's eternal divinity, and death will be forever conquered in his own eternal life.

6. Living Life to the Full

Several years ago, a ninety-four-year-old widow died in her third-floor room in a house on Jackson Boulevard in Chicago. She was widely known as a collector of antiques, and the administrator of her estate found an astonishing collection. There was a fifty-year-old accumulation of valuable chinaware, paintings, unopened crates and trunks, piled so high they crowded the ceiling. In a River Forest mansion that this woman had purchased in 1932 were twenty more rooms full of antique furniture.

A fortune in diamonds was found unexpectedly in the false bottom of a trunk. A desk or two gave up $5,000 in cash and $2,200 worth of uncashed money orders and checks. Several hundred dollars' worth of money orders had been kept so long they were unredeemable locally and had to be sent to Washington for redemption. Many of the uncashed checks were so old they were worthless under the ten-year statute of limitations. The writers of some had died or disappeared.

What would you have done, had all those treasures been yours? You would have cashed the checks, redeemed the money orders, and invested the money. You would not have missed a single opportunity to better your situation.

Many folks remind me of this eccentric widow. They leave their privileges and promises in God wholly unredeemed. Centuries ago, Jesus said, "I have come that they may have life, and have it to the full" (John 10:10 NIV). How many people do you know who are really living life to the full? There are indeed some who live out of the rich overflow of God's grace. They go forward expectantly, inspired and motivated by the indwelling presence of Christ, optimistic and enthusiastic about their future in God.

On the other hand, you probably know dozens of Christians whose lives are drab with monotony. They dream no great dreams, follow no bright guiding stars, invest themselves in no worthy causes. For them, life is but a meaningless round of existence in which they seem totally unaware of Christ's willingness and ability to change things for the better.

William James once compared our position in the universe to that of a dog in an ornate Victorian drawing room: Just as the dog is surrounded by a world of experiences, values, and powers entirely beyond its comprehension, so there is around us a world of ideas and powers that few of us are ever able to comprehend.

Let's apply the illustration. Here is a young fellow who has everything he needs by way of talents and ability to make his mark in the world. Yet with golden opportunity knocking at his door, he dawdles, wastes his time, squanders his talents, works at a job that just anyone could do. You say impatiently to yourself, "Why doesn't he wake up? Why doesn't he take hold of the advantages life offers?" You know he is far from living his life to the full and you long to arouse him to action.

But are you living your life to the full? Do you suppose there are undeveloped talents or abilities still dormant within you? A friend of mine majored in mathematics in college, expecting to teach that subject later on. But when there was no demand for mathematics instructors at the school where he served, he entered the door that was open and has served significantly in the instruction of young musicians.

The inspiration of Christ's abiding presence often opens up within us new areas of talent. A certain businessman had never won a soul to Christ until he was sixty-five and retired from industry. Since that time, he has won dozens of people to the Lord. You are never too old for something new in God. Pity the Christian whose boat remains tied to the pier when there is such a vast ocean of God's love, grace, and service to explore.

Most of us experience but a fraction of the joy that should be ours, a fraction of the peace we should know, a fraction of the divine guidance that is always available but unappropriated. Like Martha, we are so occupied with matters of secondary value that we cannot appreciate what the Lord is saying (Luke 10:38–42). We lack joy because we are doing nothing to deserve joy. Joy is a by-product of devotion and service.

Some time ago, you began a new life in Christ. Don't stop now: Keep walking with him! Christ would fill your life with power, radiance, and glowing victory. Why settle for less?

7. Watch Out for the World

The attraction of the world has been the downfall of many careless Christians. Don't let it happen to you.

Scrutinize the history of the church and you will see that the greatest loss to Christianity in each generation has not been at the point of doctrine, but of spirit. The early church did not apostatize until the vital spirit of Christ had evaporated through neglect and disloyalty. The big question was, How can we Christians be in the world and not of it? Those were dangerous days for the church. Unrest was everywhere.

Soon the church at Ephesus was accused of losing its first love (Rev 2:4). The church at Pergamum, while still holding to old truths, attempted to intermingle with these truths heretical doctrines and idolatrous practices (Rev 2:12–16). The same was true of the church at Thyatira (Rev 2:18–29). The church at Sardis was warned to renew its zeal and enthusiasm for vital things (Rev 3:1–6), and nearly the same warning was given to the church at Laodicea (Rev 3:14–22). When enthusiasm dies, carelessness sets in; and when carelessness enters, Christians tend toward the secularization of thought and a drifting away from the center of spiritual truth.

How can we draw closer to God in a world like this? The lessons of history are clear at this point. True spirituality will give way to secularism when an almost imperceptible change in motivation takes place. As a wise man warned long ago, "Keep your heart with all vigilance, for from it flow the springs of life" (Prov 4:23).

Beware when you find yourself doing religious things without your heart being in it. Beware when you find yourself praying absent-mindedly. Beware of taking your relationship with Christ for granted. If you have been a Christian for years, beware of being overtaken by a mood of self-righteousness. Keep the spiritual fire burning in your heart; keep the flames leaping high on the altar you erected for the Lord.

Stand silently sometime while the congregation around you intones the Lord's Prayer or the Apostle's Creed. When people can say, "Hallowed be your name...For the kingdom and the power and the glory are yours forever," without quickening your pulse and warming your heart, you are drifting. When you can recite, "I believe in God the Father Almighty...and in his Son Jesus Christ," with complete indifference or while watching a fly buzz in a near-by window, something has diluted the freshness of your soul. Watch the little things — the barely perceptible attitudes, the irrational prejudices. "Catch...the little foxes, that ruin the vineyards" (Song 2:15). Watch the little things and the big things will take care of themselves.

The secularizing process begins with carelessness — carelessness in making those small but vital choices, carelessness in your personal disciplines, carelessness in your stewardship obligations, carelessness in the use of your time, carelessness in the things you do and the places you go, carelessness in your conversation, carelessness in making and keeping first things first. After a time, a careless person may still believe in God but is of no earthly value to God because the soul is dead.

Years ago, a Denver fire destroyed a building that contained thousands of tons of ice. In the newspaper account, a reporter pointed out that the building contained thousands of gallons of potential fire extinguisher, but it was not in available form. It was frozen and therefore useless. Frozen assets! The church suffers today from this same tragic malady. There is plenty of talent to get the kingdom's work done, but God cannot command it; there is plenty of money in the church, but it is not at his disposal. Assets of God's kingdom have been frozen by worldliness, carelessness, neglect, lack of surrender, and the secular mood.

Here is God's will and here is your heart. Do they agree? Here are the needs of the world and here are your God-given talents. Are they available for the work of world redemption?

You will draw closer to God as you enter into a more perfect partnership with Christ.

---

8. Face Your Imperfections

The knowledge of our imperfections is enough to keep most of us at least moderately humble. What shall we do about our imperfections of character? First, it is important to face them candidly and honestly, without excuses or alibis.

A friend who has an ungovernable temper said to me, "I came by it rightly; my father had a bad temper too." As if that justified his outbursts! He will not find control until he is rid of his convenient alibi.

He ought to confess frankly, "This is my fault, and by the grace and help of God I am going to find control." All of our faults ought to be confessed and faced as readily and candidly.

How can we hope to live close to God if we permit so many things that are displeasing to him to cling to us? If we are impatient, we ought to confess it and ask for patience. We are told in the Bible to confess our faults. Perhaps we need to admit, "I'm inconsistent and undependable. I'm not as consecrated to God as I ought to be. I'm afraid of what might happen if I should really ask God to take over my life. And I'm afraid of life, death, and eternity."

Another glaring personality defect is self-pity. It is hard to help someone who feels sorry for himself. Self-pity is violently destructive to a Christian personality.

Some time ago a blind woman moved a large audience to tears with the singing of "One Sweetly Solemn Thought." In utter self-forgetfulness, she brought the presence of the living God to her inspired hearers. No one was thinking, "What a pity she is blind!" Instead they were saying, "Thank God for a living hope!" Afterward the singer said, "I have found usefulness and the greatest happiness. I have never had sight, yet God has surrounded me with a beautiful, inspiring world."

Joyful Christian living demands discipline and a great deal of tenacity. Howard M. Starratt tells of a little four-year-old boy who, one morning when snow blanketed his New England town, begged to play outside. His mother dressed him warmly and let him go, handing him a small shovel from the bucket behind the kitchen stove. Outside, this little fellow began shoveling snow from the walk, which was quite a task.

A tall stranger passing by was amused at the diminutive laborer and stopped to ask, "Just what do you think you are doing, my little man?"

The boy answered, "I'm shoveling a path for my daddy."

"And how do you expect to get it done?" the man persisted.

Straightening up, the lad looked the stranger in the eye and replied, "By just keeping at it." This is the way to succeed in the job of rounding out character — just keep at it.

It is amazing how thoroughly Christ can transform one's personality, even after conversion. Conversion is but the starting place for personality growth and improvement. Such growth should not cease as long as we live. Three young fellows made a trip into an unexplored section of the Australian interior, at last to find themselves completely surrounded by desert. At their farthest point out, one young man took a bag and filled it with soil from the desert. Back home, he planted the soil in the midst of his garden and then watched to see what would take place. Within a few days, small green sprouts appeared; strange plants began to grow. Some of them blossomed with beautiful bright red, bell-shaped flowers. Small vines, with fern-shaped foliage produced deep orange-colored flowers. Horticulturists were unable to identify them. How long these seeds had lain dormant in the desert no one knows. But placed in a more favorable environment, they sprang up in flourishing life and beauty. What potentials, what undeveloped prospects are within your soul? Furnish God with the right attitude of mind and heart and he will bring about an amazing new growth and development within you.

Some Christians cease to grow because they are altogether too satisfied for their relationship with Christ. Who wants to be an average Christian? The level is too low! Are you content to dwell at that level? Then that is where you will remain.

Handball is my favorite sport, and I have played it in YMCA gymnasiums across the country for twenty-five years. Very early, I found that I had to play frequently against my superiors in the game in order to improve my game. A player grows careless when opposed only by "dubs." If you would improve your Christian experience, associate with and follow the example of the saintliest and best people you know — folks who have a living, vital faith in God; who know how to pray and trust; who are kind and forgiving, understanding, long-suffering, loving, helpful, diligent workers in the church, backers of the program.

If you have personality defects that need remedying, take time to listen to God, for he knows best how to lead you from weakness to strength. Don't doubt it — God can get his message across to those who are really desirous to live closer to him.

---

9. "But Wanting to Justify Himself..."

Alibis and self-pity are not the only enemies of Christian stability and progress. Another is the habit of rationalizing — that is, of substituting an

42

apparently reasonable excuse for unreasonable conduct. When we deliberately justify ourselves for wrong stands, wrong attitudes, or wrong conduct, we quickly frustrate spiritual progress. In fact, we make retrogression very easy.

Luke tells us of the lawyer who stood up to tempt Jesus, saying, "Teacher, …what must I do to inherit eternal life?" But in his attempt to trap Jesus, he laid a net for his own feet. Read the conversation in the tenth chapter of Luke. Jesus gave him a very excellent answer. Then verse 29 tells us, "But wanting to justify himself, he asked Jesus, 'And who is my neighbor?'" This laid the foundation for the story of the Good Samaritan, which snared the unsuspecting lawyer in a sharp trap. Unwilling to confess he was wrong, the lawyer began to justify himself for the stand he had taken.

Honest people do not seek to justify themselves when they are shown to be wrong. When caught in a blunder (and who isn't occasionally?), do you insist that you are entirely innocent? That isn't quite honest, is it?

The apostle Peter hadn't held up too well during Christ's trial and crucifixion. In fact, he had miserably failed the Master and was no doubt very much aware of the fact. Following the resurrection, the disciples and Jesus ate dinner together and, in the relaxed quiet that followed, Jesus suddenly turned to Peter and said, "Simon son of John, do you love me more than these?" A bit bewildered by the question, Peter answered, "Yes, Lord; you know that I love you." Silence again — but all of the disciples were at attention. Jesus repeated the question a second time, and then a third. To Peter it was more than embarrassing; it was downright humiliating. By now, this impulsive but lovable disciple was squirming. How could he divert their gaze from himself?" He blurted out, "Lord, what about him?," indicating John (John 21:14–21). Peter was like most of us, anxious to justify himself.

Every nation in United Nations seems bent on justifying some stand it has taken, right or wrong. Students seek to justify their failure to make good grades by suggesting that the teacher is prejudiced or unfair or gave the examination on materials that had not been covered in class. The defeated athlete feels compelled to explain carefully how it was certainly not his fault that the game was lost. Little Johnny must explain to Mother, very convincingly, that the fight was all Jimmy's fault, even though Jimmy was an innocent bystander when the trouble began.

Sometimes we are like that. Why? Because we are embarrassed by the facts and wish to save face. We want to stand high without deserving to stand high.

In my study, a young man explained, "If you had known my parents you would understand why my marriage is failing."

Not long ago a middle-aged woman said very seriously, "We would be in church every Sunday, but I haven't been feeling at all well of late." (I happened to know that during the same period she hadn't missed a single club meeting and had attended every local basketball game.)

"I would be glad to take a box of offering envelopes, Pastor, but times are uncertain and I'm not sure I could see the year through on a pledge."

"I would be glad to forgive him, Pastor, if he would ask me to."

The closer we live to God, the less we will seek justification for our faults, failures, and sub-Christian attitudes. We will go to God honestly for help in correcting them.

A fellow once said to me, "I never apologize. An apology is a sign of weakness." He was wrong! An apology, when due, is rather a sign of meekness—a Christlike spirit. Even Christians must sometimes sing,

> Just as I am without one plea,
> But that Thy blood was shed for me;
> And that Thou bid'st me come to Thee,
> O Lamb of God, I come, I come.
> (Charlotte Elliott)

46

"For all who exalt themselves will be humbled, and those who humble themselves will be exalted" (Luke 14:11). God's way up is down!

10. What to Do with Your Troubles

This same honest, humble attitude must be maintained in the face of trouble if you would draw your best help from God. You can be sure that trouble will come; it comes to us all. Some folks seem to think that Christians should have no troubles, but the New Testament doesn't say this. The difference between a Christian and others is that the Christian has divine aid in facing troubles.

Paul wrote, "No testing has overtaken you that is not common to everyone" (1 Cor 10:13). Think of it: No trouble comes to us that has not been faced by others. Are you filled with anxiety over world conditions?

Are things going wrong in your home, or is neighborhood tension mounting over a problem involving you? Has your boy, far from home, failed to write? Are bills due and you haven't the money to pay them? Are you facing retirement and unready for it? Does your love go unrequited? Are your favors unappreciated? Everyone has troubles, but the important thing is how we face them.

A pastor said to a young woman stricken with infantile paralysis, "Affliction does so color life!"

She replied, "Yes, and I intend to choose the colors!" Brave, intelligent soul!

Affliction does color life: but you too have the power to choose what the colors will be. Listen to Paul: "Therefore, to keep me from being too elated, a thorn was given me in the flesh, a messenger of Satan to torment me, to keep me from being too elated. Three times I appealed to the Lord about this, that it would leave me, but he said to me, 'My grace is sufficient for you, for power is made perfect in weakness.'... Therefore I am content with weaknesses, insults, hardships, persecutions, and calamities for the sake of Christ; for whenever I am weak, then I am strong" (2 Cor 12:7–10).

As growing Christians, we can learn to use hardship, trouble, sickness, disappointment, and sorrow for the good of our souls, for the glory of God, and for the betterment and encouragement of others. God is sufficient for our need.

When you live close to the throne, you feel your divine friend's presence every minute of every day. You can face anything with the strength he supplies. His wisdom supplements yours. His love multiplies yours. If God is for us and with us, what can stand against us? The life lived in God is indestructible because it is one with God. A friend once said to Paschal, "I wish I had your belief, so that I might live your life." To which Paschal quickly replied, "If you lived my life, you would soon have my belief." When we have a faith that we exercise day after day, it will not be necessary to search frantically for it when trouble comes.

Henry Ward Beecher told of his father's prolonged illness and how it affected his mother. The family was very poor, for there were eleven children and the father's salary was only $800 a year. As the elder Beecher sat one day drinking his tea, his wife began to murmur gently, but sadly. Bills were due and she had no money; she didn't see how they were going to get along. She said she expected to die in the poorhouse. At that, her husband dropped his hand heavily upon the table. His eyes sparkled as he said, "My dear, I have trusted God for forty years, and I am not going to begin to doubt him now." Said Henry Ward Beecher, "That woke me up. It was better than the catechism. In all my own sickness, poverty, and trouble, I have not forgotten that scene, nor my father's words."

Christians draw closer to God when circumstances demand extraordinary faith, and it is marvelously supplied.

11. Give God the Green Light

When Jesus in the garden of Gethsemane prayed, "Not my will but yours be done" (Luke 22:42), he established for us a pattern by which all may achieve spiritual victory. Think what rebellion might have meant here! If we would live close to God, we must realize vividly that rebellion against God is costly at any point. We live as friends of God — or enemies.

In Galatians 2:21, Paul wrote, "I do not nullify the grace of God." We must make this a motto for our lives, underscoring it again and again. He must clear the way for the will of God to be done in our own lives, constantly. We must give God the green light, the "GO" sign in every area of our thought, activity, influence, and ambitions.

You and I must live the Christian life in an unchristian society, where sin and wickedness are the rule. They color everything in our environment — the newspapers, magazines, casual conversation, the humor on radio and television, other amusements and leisure time activities. It costs something to stand up for the right in days like these. When a young friend of mine rebuffed a smutty story the other day, the narrator sneeringly remarked, "When did you start wearing a halo?" God help us if we lose our Christian sense of indignation over evil!

When the Japanese Christian leader Kagawa returned to America after an absence of ten years, a college sophomore said to him, "I suppose you know that faith in Christ has busted up?" To which Kagawa calmly replied, "Mine hasn't."

Spiritual victory is not a mass movement. Every Christian must stand alone before God. Failure may be all around you, but in spite of it all, you can experience constant victory.

So many Christians are lacking in victory and joy because they frustrate the grace of

God. There are "Christian" homes where husband and wife are in a state of continual bickering. Isn't there a better way to live? Can't we endure at least a few disagreeable things for Christ's sake? Of course we can, for God's grace is sufficient for every need. We are in the world, but — thank God! — we don't have to be like it.

Live close to God, friend. We owe it to God and humanity to live with the radiance of Christ.

We must never be satisfied with less than what Christ offers us. You have heard the old story of the sea voyager who starved on crackers while crossing the ocean because he did not know that three meals a day had been included in his ticket. Let's not make that mistake. There is no need for us to be emaciated, sickly, weak Christians. There is plenty of the Bread and Water of Life for all our needs. Come, pull your chair up to the Father's table.

12. The Cost of Living Closer to God

The Sermon on the Mount is one of the greatest statements of fundamental truth ever given to man. In Matthew 5–7 is set forth in miniature the great, sweeping scope of the kingdom of God. After speaking of such basic things as meekness, mercy, purity, the desire for righteousness, right attitudes toward enemies, control of anger, getting along with people, and other kindred matters, Jesus said, "If your right eye causes you to sin, tear it out and throw it away...And if your right hand causes you to sin, cut it off and throw it away; it is better for you to lose one of your members than for your whole body to go into hell." (Matt 5:29–30). The chapter is a forceful introduction to the need for spiritual disciplines.

However, do not take these two verses literally. Gouging out an eye or cutting off a hand cannot possibly produce moral and spiritual regeneration. The seat of sin is far deeper—in the heart. Jesus is using a figure of speech to teach a lesson we Christians should learn well: If you find yourself caught in the meshes of moral or spiritual difficulties, you should be willing to pay any price to find a full restoration of your relationship with God.

Albert Cliffe tells of a successful businessman who was completely defeated in his private life. His faith in God was not vital, and he was withholding himself from the program of the church. His home life was very unhappy; he and his wife were forever at loggerheads. There was no wickedness in the man; he just couldn't get along with his wife. When divorce seemed inevitable, he decided to see Cliffe.

The two men prayed earnestly together, and in the process a new spiritual strength was found and a new vision was given. This man's wife observed the change in him immediately and inquired as to the source of it. When he explained, she too went to Cliffe for counseling and prayer and received the spiritual help she needed. As a result, this home was completely renovated by Christ, who had been neglected.

When we try to run our own lives, we wreck them. When we make Christ the head of the house, family members live together in peace and harmony. But each must work at the daily job of living close to God.

When we live close to God, it shows in everything we do. Religious educators tell us that "religion is caught, not taught." What we are often counts for far more than anything we say.

To live close to God means to look for the best in others. The benevolent, kindly, Christian attitude toward neighbors will ward off many an altercation. Someone has said, "If we understood all, we would forgive all." There is much truth in the statement. The closer we live to God, the less suspicious we will be of others. Someone who is trustworthy quickly learns to trust. It is the untrustworthy, in the main, who are most suspicious of others.

A farmer arose in a prayer meeting to witness for Christ, as others before him had done. Said he, "Every time I got down to pray, something slapped me in the face." Years earlier, he had purchased some hay from a neighbor and before he could pay for it, the neighbor died. Since the administrator of the estate knew nothing of the transaction, the bill remained unpaid. But this farmer's conscience could not rest. He finally went to the heirs and settled the account with interest. "Now," said he, "I can pray in peace." Now his testimony rang true and clear.

Every Christian wants to have a positive influence for Christ. A boy said to his mother, "When I grow up, I'm going to be a Christian just like Dad. Nobody knows whether he is a Christian or not." There is something better for us than that. And we'll find it, more and more, as we draw closer and closer to the heart of God.

13. Live Close to the Bible

Saintly Christians have invariably saturated their souls in the living Word. Thousands of Christians are today languishing instead of flourishing because they neglect the Bible.

The Bible is a book of strength, a book of guidance, a book of promise, a book inspiring high courage and faith. Revealed in its holy pages is the secret of grace.

The more you read the Bible with reverent mind, the more you will be convinced of its supernatural nature and origin. People said of Jesus, "Never has anyone spoken like this!" (John 7:46). It could likewise be said of the Bible, "There was never another book like this."

The Bible speaks with an authority that outlasts the ages. Read it daily and you will discover why Daniel Webster exclaimed after an extended study of the Gospels, "Those are the words of more than mortal men."

The Bible is in many ways a simple book; yet it is so profound that the most brilliant student can peruse it for a lifetime and at the end feel he has no more than scratched the surface of its revelations. Yet children can follow its teachings, and "no traveler, not even fools, shall go astray" (Isa 35:8) when exploring it.

The Bible has a changeless message for the changing ages—a message for every nation and race, regardless of its background or culture. The message of the Bible is sufficient for the spiritual needs of people in all walks of life.

Neglect the Bible and you neglect life. To ignore it is like a thirsting man turning away in delirium from a flowing fountain. The timelessness of the Bible and the universality of its appeal impress us again and again with the divinity of its source. The Bible is never out of date. Some portions of the Bible were written nearly thirty-five hundred years ago, yet its message is as fresh as tomorrow morning's headlines. It speaks to the living and the dying, to people who aspire, and to those whose vision is yet to be awakened. Civilizations have come and gone. Cultures have risen and disappeared. Governments have appeared and faded away, but the living Word endures forever.

Although the Bible was written over a period of perhaps fifteen hundred years, its separate parts fit together like the pieces of a jigsaw puzzle. It was written by more than thirty-five authors in at least three languages. Those who penned its sacred pages came from widely varying cultures, yet its sixty-six books complement one another. How can we account for it, except to admit that "men and women moved by the Holy Spirit spoke from God" (2 Pet 1:21)?

The French philosopher Voltaire said the Bible was a dying book and would be unremembered in a hundred years. But before the hundred years had passed, Voltaire's' own books were discredited, his home was a distribution center for the

Bible, and his own presses were being used to print this holy Book.

More than thirty million copies of the Bible, or portions of it, are sold every year. It is the world's perennial best seller. It lives on and on because men and women love the Word and treasure it in their hearts, because it gives hope to the hopeless, strength to the weak, and courage to the fearful. When "the heavens will pass away with a loud noise, and the elements will be dissolved with fire" (2 Pet 3:10), the Bible will still hold you fast in the embrace of a loving God. Trust this Book implicitly, for it will never fail you. Treasure its truth as a miser hoards his gold.

Walk by the Bible! Live by the Bible! Love and cherish the Bible, for it is the only sure guide through a world where so many have lost their way. To live close to the Bible is to live close to God.

14. Love the Truth

A college professor who was setting up an examination suggested that the students leave every other seat vacant, "in order," said he, "that you may avoid all appearance of evil."

A smart aleck held up his hand to ask facetiously, "What if we don't believe in the Good Book?"

"Then put two seats between you," the teacher retorted.

A love for truth is a regulator of the spiritual life. To some degree at least, a person is purified through a love for truth, just as a person's life is enriched through a love of beauty.

Wise leaders have always acknowledged the power of the written Word to reveal the truth. When a British monarch is crowned, the Archbishop of Canterbury takes a book and places it in the hands of the new king or queen, saying, "We present you with this Book, the most valuable thing the world affords. Here is Wisdom; this is the Royal Law; these are the lively oracles of God." The Book is, of course, the Bible. John Richard Green makes this comment regarding the Puritan period:

> England became the people of a book, and that book was the Bible. It was as yet the one English book which was familiar to every Englishman; it was read at churches and read at home, and everywhere its words, as they fell on ears which custom had not deadened, kindled a startling enthusiasm...
>
> ...The whole temper of the nation felt a change. A new conception of life and of man superseded the old. A new moral and religious impulse spread through every class.[2]

---

2. John Richard Green, *A Short History of the English People* (New York: American Book Company, 1916), 460, 462.

How different the course of America would have been, had our founders rejected the Bible! Truth makes for righteousness and progress. Nations and individuals reject freedom when they reject the truth, and there is no true progress of human civilization when truth is denied.

This does not mean that we have the truth simply because we own a Bible. To be valuable, the Bible must be read, studied, meditated upon, put into practice. Every Christian should diligently study the Word.

E. Stanley Jones once said, "I am not afraid men will be scientific: I am only afraid they will not be scientific enough." Half-truths are dangerous, but the whole truth makes for life.

Many Christians have but an inherited religion. They haven't the slightest idea why they are with this group instead of another. They are illiterate so far as the Bible is concerned. Their likes and dislikes are based on prejudices that have run in their family for generations. Their theology had been handed down, not from the Bible, but from father to son, and has picked up all manner of outside things in the process.

How can we live closer to God if we are ignorant of truth? How can we know the truth without a personal, intensive study of the Bible? Christians need to know in whom they have believed. We need to be able to give an answer for our hope. Let's not be parrot Christians, mouthing doctrines we have never thought out for ourselves, because there are no shortcuts to a knowledge of the truth. Read the Bible. As you do, ask God for understanding and guidance.

15. God Can Make His Will Known to You

Most of the counseling we pastors do is with people who either wish to know the will of God or, knowing it, have wandered and desire to regain their footing in the right path. Can you find and be guided in God's way?

A person who is constantly transgressing God's laws cannot expect clear guidance at this point. As Romans 12:1–2 indicates, only the dedicated heart is capable of judging "what is the will of God...what is good and acceptable and perfect." Obedience sensitizes the believer's conscience.

Expect God's way to be one that is in complete accord with the Spirit of Christ and the teachings of the New Testament. Expect it to be a way that leads you to bless others. Remember, God's way is always in harmony with his own spiritual principles. He never guides us to do wrong or questionable things. His ways are always right and good.

When you seek God's guidance, use every means to see your situation clearly. Sift your predicament for facts. This will often reveal how to proceed. In your search, God will probably confront you with a variety of choices. How you choose will depend upon your talents, your knowledge of your present abilities and past experiences, humanity's needs, and your own dedication.

God may give you guidance through the wise counsel and advice of intelligent, spiritually minded Christian friends. God may also bring about certain changes in the situation troubling you, thus clarifying the direction you should take.

Moses turned his back upon Pharaoh's court because he sensed God was was speaking to his heart. Every human ambition would have led this stalwart, intelligent young Hebrew in the opposite direction. His experience proves that anyone who seeks "holy ground" will find it. Anyone who wishes to know and do the will of God will have that will fulfilled. Our part is to be humble, submissive, and obedient. God will do the rest.

Maintain a Christian spirit, even toward your enemies, as you seek God's will. Hard feelings throw askew the needle of the compass by which God would lead you. Any carnal attitude may keep you from rightly knowing God's will.

God cannot guide any of us if we have already made up our minds and are praying only for his approval of our choice. An old Scotswoman used to tramp about the country, selling household goods. Since she had no particular route, when she came to a crossroads she was in the habit of tossing a stick into the air. She would then take whatever direction the stick pointed when it fell. One day, she was seen tossing the stick several times. When pressed for an explanation, she said the road to the right looked uninviting, so she had decided to just kept on tossing the stick it until pointed to the left. Are you seeking to know the will of God after this fashion?

Don't be too impatient to know what lies ahead. When you need definite direction, it will be given. John H. Jowett said he was once in a most pitiful quandary. In his need, he consulted with a trusted friend in ministry, Charles A. Berry, of Wolverhampton.

"Dr. Berry," he asked, "what would you do if you were in my place?"

His friend answered, "I don't know. I am not there, and you may not be there yet. When do you have to act?"

"Friday," Jowett replied.

"Then," said Berry, "you will find your way perfectly clear on Friday. The Lord will not fail you."

That is exactly what happened. When Friday came, Jowett had his answer.

Live close to God. Put your trust squarely in him. Be thoroughly committed to do his will and he will never fail to give you guidance. He will be your pillar of cloud by day and your pillar of fire by night.

---

16. How Far Will You Go for God?

Some people are afraid to take even slight risks, despite the prospect of rich rewards. They say, "I'll never travel in the mountains; it's too dangerous." Or, "Don't expect me to board an ocean liner; too much can happen out there." Or, "You couldn't hire me to go up in an airplane."

Other people enjoy challenges. What is more thrilling than to set out on a five-mile path through evergreens and ice-cold lakes, leading to the pinnacle of a mountain just as the eastern sky is being set a fire by the rising sun? Or to stand on the deck of a forty-foot cabin cruiser as it turns its head into a blow? Or to look down from an elevation of fifteen thousand feet upon a perfect sea of clouds, with the sun shining down gloriously upon them while you hurtle along through space at more than three hundred miles an hour?

If we are to be Christians worthy of the name, we must be willing to respond to challenges, assume risks, and keep going when the way is rough. We must be willing to go the second mile—and even the third—on behalf of Christ and his kingdom. God is looking for courageous, obedient servants who will dare, with the three Hebrew young men, to face danger with steadfast hearts. Even with their lives in direct peril, those young men said to King Nebuchadnezzar, "If our God whom we serve is able to deliver us from the furnace of blazing fire and out of your hand, O king, let him deliver us. But if not, be it known to you, O king, that we will not serve your gods and we will not worship the golden statue that you have set up" (Dan 3:17–18).

What divinely inspired audacity they displayed! What courage and faith! The prickles must have been running up and down their spinal columns as they took their stand. But take their stand they did, and God stood by them! They were not forced to thus risk their lives. They could have taken the easy way of compromise, the way of the crowd. No one is forced to go a little farther. It takes something extra inside a person to live the "plus" kind of life for God — something you receive only by living closer to him.

Remember, however, that those who have had that something extra made history — Jesus, Peter, Stephen, John Hus, John Knox, Martin Luther, John Wesley. Their second-mile faith blesses us even today. They lived lives that made a difference. How many Christians are of that caliber today? How many second- and third-mile Christians do we have in this generation? Who today is willing to go a little farther for Christ?

A flock of geese used to gather in a corner of the barnyard once every week to hear one or more of their number speak eloquently about the glory of flying. They imagined the thrill of soaring through the air at express-train speed, of feeling the bite of the cold wind in their faces, of how beautiful the lakes and rivers would appear when viewed from the heights. All would enthusiastically agree and fan their wings in applause — after which they would placidly and contentedly go back to their feed troughs without ever trying to fly.

Are any of us like that? Do we go to church once a week to hear a wonderful sermon about the glories of daring service in God's kingdom, only to go back home and do nothing about it? If you would live closer to God, spread your wings and venture into an area that is unknown to you. If you have decided to climb no more mountains, sail no more seas, and enter no more battles for the Lord, then your future is all in the past.

Have you ever noticed the affinity clouds have for mountain peaks? I saw Mount Fujiyama clearly only once during a month in Japan because every day a cloud nestled about this twelve-thousand-foot peak. Someone has said great souls are like mountains: They always attract storms; upon their heads break the thunders and around them the lightnings flash. If you are afraid of storms, stay out of the mountains. If you are afraid of dedication, work, and complete surrender to the purposes of God, stay away from the cross. Unless you are willing to accept unusual challenges, stay away from Gethsemane, for people suffer there and are sometimes led directly from the garden to the cross. But a word of caution: if you withhold yourself from Christ, you will always hate yourself for it.

Dare to be an extraordinary Christian! Forgive your enemy quickly, without being asked. Consider all material things under your control as belonging to God. (He is the owner: You are but a steward operating under his direction.) See yourself as his partner in the work of taking the gospel into the entire world.

Perhaps the reason some of us are a bit difficult at times is because our religion is not of the second-mile quality. We need to deepen our consecration. We need to go a little farther with the Lord.

---

17. God Is at Work in You

Why does this challenge to live closer to God cause uneasiness? God never asks the impossible of us, and with every command he furnishes the necessary grace and strength to carry out his desires. When we go forward at Christ's order, a divine presence goes with us to give success to the endeavor. In this connection, J. B. Phillips offers an interesting rendition of Philippians 2:13, "For it is God Who is at work within you, giving you the will and the power to achieve His purpose." This declaration has rather thrilling implications for us all. It means that God is at work within you — to control your mind, illuminate your heart, direct your activities, broaden the scope of your Christian influence, and in general make your life more effective than it otherwise could be.

If God is really at work in you, what is he doing?

First, he is seeking to draw you nearer and nearer to himself. He desires an intimate personal relationship with you. For that relationship to be unhindered, he would remove all of your personality defects and replace them with positive, helpful fruits of the Spirit. He is refining your spirit and improving of your total being. As he works, you become a more capable and a more lovable person because he lives within you.

Second, God is influencing your activities, just as an efficient general manager influences the activities of a factory or office. You see the manager's influence in improvements, increased efficiency, and the creation of a better product. God is at work in you to do this same thing. If you put him in full control of your life, remarkable changes will take place. Benevolent urges that move you to deeds of Christian kindness and service will increase in number and intensity. You will be more keenly aware of opportunities to speak a word of comfort or invitation to those about you. You will know better what to say to best advantage. Your values will become more and more Christian. Greater power will be given you in times of temptation and stress. God strengthens the bulwarks of your human spirit against all evil.

Third, God is aligning your attitudes with those of his own divine mind. "Let the same mind be in you that was in Christ Jesus" (Phil 2:5). Think what this means to your home relationships, business dealings, and social contacts! Think how this can enable you to deal with problems which engender strife in our modern world, such as international difficulties, race problems, and labor unrest. Suppose all of these problems were approached from both sides of the negotiating table with the mind of Christ at work in every heart. How quickly and well all disputes would be settled!

Fourth, God is moving you to show tenderness and compassion. God is at work in you when you forgive a wrong, when you refuse to hold a grudge, or when you ignore an insult. God is at work in you when you bring your tithes and offerings into his storehouse. He is at work in you when you deny yourself for the sake of his kingdom, when you control your tongue, when you bring your natural human desires under the control of the Holy Spirit. God is at work in you when your motives and ambitions come to be centered in his will and purposes for you.

Fifth, God is helping others through you. Dick Sheppard tells of his first attempt to minister in the impoverished East End of London some years ago. He was a cocksure university student, full of zeal to set the world right, sure he had all the answers to life's problems. He was given the task of trying to share the gospel with a drunkard, but his talks with the poor man seemed to do no good and made little impression.

After an absence of several weeks, Dick visited him again and found that the inebriate had signed a total abstinence pledge and was keeping it. In Sheppard's absence, a little-known parish clergyman named Strickland had called on the alcoholic. Strickland was shy. Often the two men would just sit in the room for long periods of time without saying a word. But one day when Strickland had gone, the alcoholic said to his wife, "It's just as though Jesus Christ had been sitting in that chair." The drunkard's life was changed because God reached him through the heart of a humble clergyman.

God works through the heart that cares! He may use you to bring salvation, not only to the souls of other people, but to their minds and bodies also. He may use you to provide them with good Christian literature that sets forth plainly the way of redemption through Christ.

God needs followers who allow him to work through their dedicated hearts and talents to perfect his will for the whole human race. A certain amount of God's work will never be done if you fail in your trust. Certain lives will never be touched by the gospel unless you take it to them. But if you move forward with faith to fulfill God's purpose, you will never walk or work alone.

18. Pray—to Find God

The following chapters on prayer are of vital significance to all who would live closer to God, for the most direct route to the throne of God is through prayer. Hundreds of books have been written on the subject, and hundreds will yet be written. This is because prayer is the essence of worship and devotion and is the chief means of communication between God and us.

There are various reasons to pray, and one of the most fundamental is the need to know God. Job exclaimed, "Oh, that I knew where I might find him!" (Job 23:3). Job was wretched and miserable because he felt estranged from the divine presence. There is no more vexing frustration than to fall short in your quest to find God. What is more exasperating than nearly to find him and then fail?

Many people seek God by meditating upon the beauties of nature, but there is a better way by which to find God; that is through believing prayer. The beauties of nature are the products of God, but they are not God. We are not pantheists. God is greater than all his acts of creation, and he is greater than the sum total of all his wonderful attributes.

Can we know God himself? Yes, we can! Remember that Jesus prayed in John 17, "And this is eternal life, that they may know you, the only true God, and Jesus Christ whom you have sent" (v. 3). So we can know the unknowable. In many ways, God cannot be known; but in ways vital to our spiritual life and progress, he can be known. And the search for God must begin on bended knee.

The Church of the Nativity at Bethlehem can be entered through but one door, and it is no more than three or four feet high, so that everyone who enters must stoop — bend the knee — to do so. It is thus in prayer also. No careless search for God will be rewarded. No halfway desire will bring us into the divine presence. Thoughtless and insincere petitions will be to little or no avail. Yes, you will find traces of God in nature. You will find him more fully revealed in the Bible. You will see him as you read the history of the church. You will observe him today in the lives of saintly people. But God is found best when your heart is attuned to him in humble, reverent, believing prayer.

Ours is a world of doubt, suspicion, distrust, and fear. Perhaps you know what mental torture is involved when you begin to mistrust someone you love. It is sheer anguish. Some Christians were converted decades ago, yet they still struggle with doubts and fears about God. This condition ought not to exist. Isn't it strange that adults often struggle where children relax in trusting faith? Perhaps Jesus had this in mind when he said, "Unless you change and become like children, you will never enter the kingdom of heaven" (Matt 18:3).

Pray to trust God's love. For if God does not represent love to you, he is not real. David said, "Evening and morning and at noon I utter my complaint and moan, and he will hear my voice" (Ps 55:17). Have full confidence that God hears and answers your prayer.

Years ago, Richard Cameron of the Boston University School of Theology built a lovely home at Concord, Massachusetts. In the basement, he had the usual recreation room, but over to one side, he built a small chapel. This family chapel had an altar and various symbols to stimulate reverence and worship. Into this place, Cameron brought his children for daily prayer, and in the quiet hush of meditation and communion, they found God. In the years that followed, it became as natural for them to worship in the chapel as to play ping-pong in the game room.

When prayer becomes this natural, our lives are undergirded with a divine power that will never fail us.

---

19. Pray—to Be Like Christ

One prayer that should be offered daily is a prayer to be like Christ. Peter said we should follow in the steps of the Savior. Charles M. Sheldon wrote a great book about it. But no person can live like Christ without first being transformed into his image.

Prayer can put us in harmony with God's will. When we live according to his will, he can work through us. Victorious personal power comes as the result of that harmonious relationship.

At the tomb of Lazarus, Jesus prayed, "Father, I thank you for having heard me [although nothing had happened thus far]. I knew that you always hear me, but I have said this for the sake of the crowd standing here, so that they may believe that you sent me" (John 11:41–42). Christ's spotless life gave him absolute confidence that God heard him when he prayed.

John wrote, "Beloved, if our hearts do not condemn us, we have boldness before God; and we receive from him whatever we ask, because we obey his commandments and do what pleases him" (1 John 3:21–22). What was the condition? "If our hearts do not condemn us." Faith is weakened when it is necessary to pray from a condemned heart; it is strengthened when all is clear between us and God. Deliberate transgression alienates us from God. He can forgive sin but never condone it.

Pray to be like Jesus so that your divine fellowship can be maintained. Pray for his love, mercy, and Spirit. To be like Christ is to love. When you violate the high law of love, you make it impossible for Christ to give you spiritual growth.

Such love is never possessive, but always seeks to give more than it receives. It never says, "my way," but, "Thy way." Self must die, so that Christ may live in its place. Two cannot occupy a throne at the same time. Will it be self or Christ?

If you are like Christ, you will be forgiving. We are unforgiven ourselves until we forgive others. "If you do not forgive others, neither will your Father forgive your trespasses" (Matt 6:15).

Pray to have the mind of Christ, to think his thoughts, to be guided by his judgment. Let yourself see the world as Christ saw it. Let his love of little children be yours. Let his compassion for the poor be yours. He cared when people were ill, tired, and downtrodden. Do we have his attitude toward our enemies? Toward money and other material things? Do we see the ungodly through the mind and eyes of Christ? You and I are human beings and woefully subject to error, but our errors will be much fewer in number if we pray to have the mind of Christ in all our judgments.

When Jesus was faced with a problem, he prayed. When he had been blessed with outstanding success, he prayed. We should follow his example. We should not let anything interfere with our prayer life.

Glenn Clark said he quit taking the morning paper for twelve years because it interfered with his morning quiet time. He thought it more important to hear from God at the beginning of the day than to read the news headlines. When we have that deep a desire to walk with God, we will always find him ready and waiting, out there where the path begins.

---

20. Pray—Because Prayer Changes Things!

A preacher was being driven to an appointment by a fellow who was full of criticism of everything and everybody. He criticized the weather and the condition of the country and then began to relate what was wrong with his wife. Arriving at their destination, the preacher said, "Come into this little room with me and we will talk some more."

When the door was shut, the driver blurted out, without any prompting, "What's wrong with me?"

"You tell me," the preacher said.

The man broke down and wept. He finally asked, "How can I become a different person?"

"Do you believe Jesus Christ can change you?" the preacher asked.

Thoroughly chastened, the man answered, "With all my heart. I want to be a different person."

They got down on their knees, but the man said he couldn't pray. He protested that he didn't know how. The preacher instructed him as he would a child, saying, "All right, you say what I say."

At the preacher's prompting, the man prayed, "Dear Lord, take all the meanness out of my heart. Set me free from myself. I don't want to be this way any more. Please change me. Amen." At that point, he forgot he didn't know how to pray and began to tell the Lord a great many things. When they arose from prayer, the driver was a transformed man. God did it in response to his sincere prayer.

Ask God to bring about any change that needs to be made in your life. He can do it. You don't need to use impressive words; just confess what you think is wrong and ask God to help you make it right. It is that simple! Kermit Olsen said that the most earnest prayer he ever heard consisted of two words, "Oh, God!" Just talk to God as a child would talk to an understanding, loving father. Put your yearning into words if you can, because it helps to clarify the situation in your own thinking. Remember, however, that God doesn't depend upon your words. He knows your heart!

Be very honest and frank in confessing your needs. Don't hold back anything from God. Refusal to confess fully your needs is proof that a bit of pride still lingers in your heart. Frank prayer clears the way of obstructions, opening a channel for divine grace to enter. It aligns your changeable will to God's unchanging character.

It is amazing how prayer can change your whole outlook. Troubles appear in a different light after you have laid them out before God in prayer. The battle you have been losing will be won when you earnestly solicit God's help in prayer, submitting your will to his purposes. Burdens that would normally crush a person are carried with ease when that person prays.

Prayer also changes relationships and social situations. Louise Harrison McCraw writes, "As we pray for others, God not only works in their hearts but He also works in ours. He makes our own hearts clean and warm. The next time we have a contact with the one prayed for, there is a power in our words, our very tones, that could have come in no other way than through former contacts with God Almighty."[3]

Pray for the person you don't like or who doesn't like you. Answers to such prayer come from God, but they also come from our own inner hearts. Some serious trouble had arisen between the president of a manufacturing concern and his employees. In the growing disunity, management began posting rules until the bulletin board was crowded with them.

---

3. Louise Harrison McCraw, *Does God Answer Prayer?* (Grand Rapids, MI: Zondervan Publishing House, 1941), 108.

The union was resentful and seething with restlessness. Then the president of the company began taking his troubles to God in prayer. As he prayed, he realized that he ought to change some of his attitudes and begin thinking of how working conditions could be improved. So he went to the head of the union with a proposition. As a result, all the rules were taken down from the bulletin boards and one simple card was posted instead, reading: "In everything do to others as you would have them do to you" (Matt 7:12). Soon peace returned to the factory. As the president would walk through various departments, he began to feel warmth and good will. The head of the union called out one day, "Hi, Bill. How's everything with you?"

Prayer works when you turn your life and problems over to God. Is there something in your life that you ought to be praying about?

21. Pray—Because God Does Answer Prayer

The closer you live to God, the more you will be convinced that God does hear and answer prayer. And the more you pray, the simpler your prayers will be. For prayer is really but a matter of placing yourself—all your needs and all your problems—trustfully in God's hands and being willing to cooperate with him to the fullest in bringing about the needed results. Our best praying is relaxed praying, in which we are keenly aware of our utter dependence upon God but believe he is interested in us and will stand by us.

Prayer at its best never insists on anything but trusts that everything we really need will be given. Prayer never threatens; it invites. We don't go to prayer to bargain with God but to find and accept his will.

A problem once arose in a congregation I was serving, and I was fearful of handling it because of its potential power to split the congregation. So I prayed and waited while for months the matter simmered. It finally reached a crisis point where something had to be done. At two o'clock in the morning, I was tossing restlessly, wide awake and praying for guidance in handling this disturbing situation. As definitely as if God had spoken audibly, the question came to mind, Whose church is this? I had to admit it was God's, not mine. Then whose problem is this? And I answered, "Yours, Lord; and you can have it. I'm going to sleep." Within twenty-four hours, that problem worked itself out without any help from me and without the loss of a single person from our church.

Prayer changes things. God does answer our needs when we send him our petitions in faith. That is old-fashioned theology, but it is true!

Strange things happen when we pray. I was called from a seminary class in Dayton, Ohio, one morning to a local hospital where a young woman lay dying. In the hall outside the room, a veteran nurse stood weeping. I stopped a moment to comfort her, not knowing the cause of her distress. She said, through tears, "I've lost my last three patients, and now the fourth is dying too. It's more than I can take." I prayed briefly for her and then entered the sickroom where a woman of thirty or so lay dying. Her mother stood by, sobbing with grief, and the young husband was almost overcome with emotion. It was difficult to quiet them for prayer. In closing my prayer, I asked, "Dear Lord, if anything can be done for this woman that the doctors haven't thought of, please bring it quickly to their attention."

Immediately, the nurse rushed in, apologized for pressing by me, and said, "The doctor just called down from surgery. He thought of one more thing he wants to try." Three weeks later, this patient stood in our church on Sunday morning as a visitor and gave thanks to God for her healing.

Are you in trouble? What is your difficulty? Whatever it is, take it to the Lord in prayer — simple, trusting, believing prayer, and expect God to help you. Pray courageously and in faith. Ask largely, but pray humbly; then rest your case confidently in the hands of God. It will amaze you what God will do.

---

22. In the Beauty of Holiness

For some time, the Old Testament injunction to "worship the Lord in the beauty of holiness" has been running through my mind. Four times this phrase appears in the New King James Version of the Holy Bible. In 1 Chronicles 16:29, we read, "Give to the Lord the glory due His name; Bring an offering, and come before Him. Oh, worship the Lord in the beauty of holiness." In 2 Chronicles 20:21, the statement is, "And when he [King Jehoshaphat] had consulted with the people, he appointed those who should sing to the Lord, and who should praise the beauty of holiness, as they went out before the army and were saying, 'Praise the Lord, for His mercy endures forever.'" Third is the passage in Psalm 29:2, "Give unto the Lord the glory due to His name; worship the Lord in the beauty of holiness." Fourth is the word in Psalm 96:8–9, "Give to the Lord the glory due His name; Bring an offering, and come into His courts. Oh, worship the Lord in the beauty of holiness! Tremble before Him, all the earth."

Other versions do not use this phrase. In Moffatt's translation, three of the four times, we read, "Worship the Eternal in festal attire." The fourth verse says, "Kneel before God in sacred vestments." Other modern versions say, "Worship the Lord in holy attire" (NASB) and "Worship the Lord in holy array" (RSV). In each case, Scripture exhorts us to worship God with the best we can offer.

There must have been a great deal of pageantry connected with public worship in Old Testament times. The richness of the temple would set the scene. The sounding of trumpets gave a regal air, while the antiphonal singing of great massed choirs would contribute to the awesome stateliness of the occasion. Over all would drift pungent smoke from burning incense. The dim interior of the temple was illuminated by burning tapers and the strikingly rich attire of the priests. Add to this the fragrance of the cedar paneling, the rich gold overlay, the extensive ritual, and you will begin to feel some of the emotion a good Jew would quickly identify with temple worship. No wonder the people were admonished to "worship the Lord in holy array" (RSV)! Worship was not an occasion to be taken lightly. Worshipers were there to honor God, and the whole atmosphere inspired holy awe and fear, filling them with a sense of God's majesty.

I fear that, as Halford Luccock suggests, some of us come to worship in our everyday working clothes: "No fresh array of wonder, of aspiration, no trembling hope…" Some come clothed in egotism and self-righteousness. Some come in judge's robes, with much criticism in their hearts. They sit in judgment on the preacher, the sermon, the music, the entire program. But not the person who sincerely strives to live close to God! This worshiper bows his head because his heart is already humbled before the Lord. He shuts out of his mind all thoughts except those related to this high hour. He bares his soul before the King as he sits lost in wonder, love, and praise.

God walks with the humble and pure in heart. He still meets at the place of prayer those whose yearning hearts aspire upward. He still bends a listening ear to the slightest whisper of the trusting soul. What privilege to worship him! What privilege to be called the children of God!

23. There Is a Sanctuary for You

Christians who avoid the church are robbing their hearts of a chief means of fellowship and grace. We find spiritual strength and growth by worshiping together, praying together, working together. Many problems have been solved as God's people sat together in a service of divine worship. In the house of God, it is easier to hear his still, small voice.

Psalm 27:4–5 says, "One thing I asked of the Lord, that will I seek after: to live in the house of the Lord all the days of my life, to behold the beauty of the Lord, and to inquire in his temple. For he will hide me in his shelter in the day of trouble; he will conceal me under the cover of his tent; he will set me high on a rock."

The church provides a warm sanctuary for every one of us. It's a place of prayer for all nations, classes, and people. It means most to those who belong to Christ and have learned to worship. However, I heard Eddie Cantor invite everyone to church at the close of one of his radio programs during World War II. He said something like this:

Here in Los Angeles a few days ago we had a rather disturbing windstorm. I was walking along Sunset Boulevard at the time, and like all pedestrians I ran for cover as a gale swept down. There were a number of stores nearby, but something guided me toward a building across the street. I stood there in the archway several minutes before I realized I was in the doorway of a church. It set me to thinking.

The world today is going through something far more threatening than a windstorm. Every single one of us needs refuge of one kind or another. And I know of no better place to go for it than to church. We are extremely fortunate to live in a country where we can worship as we please, when we please. Let's make the most of this blessing. The greatest calamity that can befall a people is the loss of religion. Don't let it happen here! Go to church.

Friend, you can find sanctuary in the church. You can live closer to God by living close to the church, for it is the body of Christ and his holy bride.

---

24. Keep Your Eyes on Jesus

Thousands of Christians have lost their faith because they took their eyes from Christ. Christ must be alive within our hearts or we will most certainly be upset, confused, and led astray by situations with which we will be confronted. Only a vital faith in him can hold us in the crisis.

These are threatening days, when the world picture is gloomy. International tensions can trouble our minds until we lose our grasp on the sustaining power of God. We can look at conditions in our own country and become faithless pessimists. The Bible warns us of such times, saying, "Wicked people and impostors will go from bad to worse, deceiving others and being deceived" (2 Tim 3:13).

All of us seek a city of refuge. We want something strong enough to bear us up in time of storm. Only the eternal Rock of Ages can do this.

On the other hand, weak Christians become even weaker as time goes by. We are painfully aware of the faults, failings, sins, and blunders of certain leaders who claim to know our Lord but do not follow conscientiously in his steps. We must not allow things like these to shake us.

Ananias and Sapphira hypocritically sought a place among the dedicated (Acts 5:1–11). A certain Simon tried to purchase spiritual power with money (Acts 8:9–24). Does this prove the church is shallow and unworthy and that Christianity is a failure? Far from it! Every so often, a preacher "goes bad." Occasionally, you find a Christian who refuses to honor his debts. You sometimes find a married couple in church who quarrel and wrangle continuously. But these things are not new. First Corinthians describes many people in the early church who were guilty of quarreling, factionalism, jealousy, strife, arrogance, immorality, boasting, and associating with bad people. These sins and faults are not characteristic of redeemed people but, we admit, can be found among the small group of hangers-on who intermingle with God's people.

This need never affect your own relationship to Christ. You must find and maintain your own personal faith in God, and this faith should not depend in the slightest degree upon the success or failure of others. You can be strong when others are weak. You can hold right attitudes, pray much, love people, stay under the control of a godly spirit, love the Word, and remain humble and obedient. The aberrations of others need not weaken you in the least. You are not held by the power of men but by the power of God. You are safest when you look after your own responsibilities and keep your eyes on Christ.

---

25. Live Closer—in Good Times and Bad

Job was not the last to inquire in time of trouble, "Where is God, my maker?" (Job 35:10). But he also knew that God gives strength in the night."

We are much like poor old Job, wondering why tragedy must strike us, why disappointment and trouble must come our way. If only life would hold to a constant pattern of happiness and blessing! But life means change, and change requires us to adapt ourselves to circumstances. Life is not all sunshine; God never meant it to be. But neither is it all storm and shadow.

Do you feel life has been hard on you? Really, what has happened to you has been happening to humanity for thousands of years, and some have fared far worse. Many of them have been the best people. Remember Daniel, that fine, resolute, godly young man who faithfully lived for God. But this very faith was responsible for getting him into trouble, even to the point that one day he found himself in a den of lions.

Another classic illustration is found in the account of Paul and Silas in the old Philippian jail. Did they sulk and grow bitter? Never! They sang and prayed together. As a result, the jailer and his entire family were converted and baptized. It takes Christian maturity and a great deal of faith to go through such trials and use them for God's glory and one's own spiritual growth.

The Bible tells us not to despise the day of small things (Zech 4:10). We must learn to crawl before we can walk, and walk before we can run. Walk with God in the day and you will find it much easier to sing with him in the long night of trouble.

When I was about fifteen, my sister and I had worked late one evening in the city of Indianapolis and finally started out from town on a Northwestern streetcar. A fog, which had been heavy in town, thickened and deepened as we rode toward home. Shortly, we were the only passengers on the car. The motorman, who was not too familiar with this run, finally said to me, "I have no idea where we are. I'm just letting the car follow the tracks. Whenever you think you are near your street, just say the word and I'll let you off."

When I thought we were near our street, I gave the signal and the car was stopped. My sister and I crossed the street, found the corner that I thought was ours, turned west, went to the end of the block, and then counted back to the fourth private entrance walk. We were home. We found our way that night in the thick fog because we were so used to coming that way in the day.

So many people never call on the Lord except in trouble and then find it hard to locate him. Walk with him when everything is going well and he will be near to help you when things go wrong.

The actor Edwin Booth were once playing in a London theater. The night was rainy and stormy, and only a few people came to see the play. Most of them sat far back, so the huge auditorium seemed deserted. A discouraged cast pleaded with Booth to postpone the performance; but he refused, saying, "We shall go on! Remember, the king sits in every audience! Play to the king!"

That night, Booth gave one of the best performances of his illustrious career. A day or two later, the king sent for Booth. It turned out that the king had actually been sitting among the few people scattered in the shadowy last rows of the theater that night, bundled up in a great coat with a high collar. How good Booth must have felt to know he had indeed played to the king!

We too need to be reminded that the King sits in every audience as we play our role in life. He is there when things go well, and he is there when life is shadowed by trouble. He is always there. So play to the King! In sunshine or shadow, in good times or bad, in happiness or grief, at noontime or midnight—play to the King! Sincere, conscientious Christians seek to be their best for God all the time.

---

26. The Joy of Conquest

My wife and I enjoyed one of our most satisfying vacations by making a leisurely trip through the golden West. But toward the end, we yearned to get back home to the work of pastoring a church.

In four weeks, we had driven across miles of desert, mountains, and green valleys. It was country made famous by the pioneers of a hundred years and more ago. Riding along excellent highways, about the only thing we shared in common with our pioneering ancestors was the ability to enjoy the unending beauty. All about us were towering mountains, rushing streams, beautiful waterfalls, majestic evergreen trees, and the limitless mesquite and sagebrush of the desert.

As we were about to head east from Portland, Oregon, an elderly man remarked, "I wish I could go back to work. You are lucky to have people who need you. And you are fortunate to have your health." He had been city engineer in a California town until a serious heart attack forced him into early retirement.

Back home again, I found new interest in reading a history of the early days of American pioneering and exploration. I read especially of Lewis and Clark, with whom I journeyed in imagination up the Missouri River to discover finally a gateway through the Rockies.

I thought of the hardships they endured. There were rivers to cross, and no bridges; mountains to conquer, and no trails; deserts, and no way of knowing how far it was to the next water hole. Yet they pushed on, inspired by their dream of conquest, invited forward by the ever-unfolding panorama of the West. They had to see what was around the next bend of the river or just beyond that distant chain of mountains.

I could almost see the stars shining down from the late evening sky, smell the smoke of the campfires, and hear the subdued strumming of a guitar as the camp settled itself for the night. The day may have been rugged, but with a good meal under their belts, these men were soon ready to set out again. They were pioneers and were blazing a new trail! The joy of conquest was upon them!

There is something invigorating about conquest. It gets into your blood. If I were a young minister again, I would go where I could start low and rise higher, where I could experience the thrill of adventure in a new field, where every bit of progress would show.

We admire the courageous heroes of Christian history who dreamed and dared and won! But most of us are armchair explorers. We are satisfied with vicarious adventures. We watch the athletic contests and shout advice, but we stay off the gridiron.

We need more Christians who are driven forward daily by an inner compulsion to serve God and their fellow believers, to give themselves to finishing the work our Lord began. We need Christians who are not afraid of hard places and tasks calling for endurance and consecration. We need Christians who have not lost their sense of daring, who are willing to work for the sake of the church, for there are no real accomplishments for the kingdom without work. "Faith by itself, if it has no works, is dead" (James 2:17).

The plain truth is this: The church is in desperate need of consecrated, trained, devoted pioneers. Your spiritual development will depend to a great extent on what you do to help fill this need. "The harvest is plentiful, but the laborers are few" (Matt 9:37).

God may need you for the ministry. Have you asked him about it? If he calls, do not be afraid to answer, "Here am I!" Some of the deepest satisfactions in the world come to the person who, called of God, is devoted to the work of ministry.

We need Christian executives to help direct the business affairs of the church. Too many times these practical business-people have been neglected because of their personalities. They are not soft; so many people judge them to be unspiritual when exactly the opposite is often true.

We need Christian politicians who will direct the affairs of the city or state in the spirit of Christ. We need public school teachers by the thousand to emanate truth, loyalty, and devotion to the Master wherever they are. We must have more and more Christian mothers who will bring up their children in the fear of God. We must have more and better-trained missionaries for the home and foreign fields. This calls for self-denial and deep devotion to humanity. We need singers and other musicians whose talents and time are thoroughly committed to God. The men's organization and women's groups need leadership and workers.

We need devoted Christians whose money and other material assets are fully dedicated to God's use. We need thousands and thousands of tithers to support liberally every phase of the outgoing work of the kingdom of God. Money is no substitute for work, but neither is work a substitute for money. It is almost impossible to live close to God without being liberal with both our time and our money.

You seldom find a growing Christian who has no special burden for at least one phase of the church's work. One has a burning zeal for missions. Another has a passion for the instruction of children. Another is interested in personal evangelism. Another feels a burden to organize the men of the church for united action in needy projects. Another sees the need for relief programs, social settlements, and missions in downtown areas of large cities. Another plunges into the rural districts of the South to help underprivileged farmers become more efficient—and, incidentally, better Christians!

In my childhood days, we had a small motto hanging on the wall of our classroom in the Sunday school, which read, "What kind of church would this church be, If every member were just like me?" I have never forgotten it. None of us should, for the church is but an aggregation of individual Christians, who must carry the work of God forward to success.

Do you think there are no more frontiers? There are! The buffalo may be gone from the Western prairie and the Indian from the plain; the rivers may all be bridged and highways traverse the highest passes in the Rockies; but the spirit of adventure is still needed in the church! Every time I visit the Rockies, I find myself wishing to live where their grandeur would always greet my eyes. I would examine every canyon, fish every stream, and climb every mountain. Nothing puts the mood of adventure in my heart as do the mountains. Nothing, that is, except ministering for Christ and the church! For the church stands for daring too; its history is aglow with stories of valiant men and women who braved everything for Christ. The church still has frontiers, canyons, rivers, and mountains. Its canyons are made by the towering walls of skyscrapers in cities where, amid the rushing thousands of busy feet, sad people walk alone. Its rivers are the streams of humanity that move on and on in search of contentment. Its mountains are the injustices, the evil, and the malpractices that call for justice in the name of Christ.

What new territory will you take for God? There you will find your greatest joy and discover anew the reason you were born, the purpose for which God brought you into this world. Go wherever the fields are ripe for harvesting. Go wherever various-colored hands are lifted in pleading supplication. God needs you—if not in a foreign country, perhaps to help the family next door.

So keep your heart open to divine guidance. Be sensitive to the moving Spirit of the Eternal. Live close to the throne. Great days are ahead for you!

27. His Steadfast Love Endures Forever

If we live close to God, he will see us through the years with victory, and at the end of life's journey, receive us to himself in peace. How thankful to God we should be for his blessings and sustaining grace! We say with David, "O give thanks to the Lord, for he is good; for his steadfast love endures forever" (Ps 106:1).

It is said that Confucius once came upon a man caught in a bed of quicksand and remarked, "There is proof that men should stay out of such places." Buddha also saw this victim and said, "Let that be a lesson to others." Mohammed observed the hapless fellow and commented, "Alas! It is the will of Allah!" A Hindu saw and called, "Cheer up, friend! You will return to earth in another form." But when Jesus saw him, he whispered, "Give me your hand, brother, and I will pull you out."

It is but a story, but it typifies the mercy of a God who cares — who cares for you! How manifold are his blessings! How grateful we should be for the sweet privilege of walking with him day after day.

Yet ingratitude is one of today's commonest sins. Samuel Leibowitz, famous as a criminal lawyer, saved seventy-eight men from the electric chair. Not a single one of them ever wrote him a letter of thanks!

Travel the journey of life with thanksgiving and praise in your heart. First, thank God for Christ and his abiding presence. Thank God for the church where you have found a fellowship rich and good. Thank God for Christian friends with whom you labor in the most important work in the world. Thank God you have a part in that work, for it is of eternal value. Thank God for faith that holds you steady and true in the face of every circumstance. Thank God for supplying your material needs. Then thank God for a living hope, for if you walk with the Lord in this world, you need have no fear of the world to come.

In Germany, a young man lay on the operating table, waiting for the surgeon to remove a cancer from his tongue. "Young man," said the doctor, "if you have anything to say, now is your opportunity, because after this operation you will never be able to speak again."

What would you have said? Tears came to the young man's eyes and, after a pause, he spoke the last words his cancerous tongue would ever form: "Thank God for Jesus Christ!"

Perhaps there is a great deal more to this matter of living close to God. But to be grateful, to love, to serve, to give, to worship and adore, to learn to pray well — these are the essence of the quest.